DESTINATION ITALIAN

**Illustrated Phrasebook
& Travel Information**

**Teresa Huntley and
Mike Buckby**

NTC Publishing Group
Lincolnwood, Illinois USA

Book and Tapescript by
Teresa Huntley
and Mike Buckby

Cassettes produced by Colette Thomson

Destination Italian was produced in collaboration with
the Language Teaching Centre at the
University of York

Illustrations by Annie Farrall

Picture credits
Alex Dufort page 71; *Robert Harding* pages 79 (Michael Short), 90 (Rolf Richardson) and 91 *bottom* (Walter Rawlings); *Image Bank* pages 67 (Guido Rossi), 88 (Michael Melford) and 91 *top* (Stockphotos/Terry Williams); *Spectrum* pages 87 and 93.

This edition first published in 1996 by
NTC Publishing Group,
4255 W. Touhy Avenue, Lincolnwood, Illinois, USA 60646-1975.
© Kate Corney and Mike Buckby 1993
Published in co-operation with BBC Worldwide Limited.
"BBC" and the BBC logotype are trademarks of the
British Broadcasting Corporation, and are used under licence.

Printed in Hong Kong.

5 6 7 8 9 0   WKT   9 8 7 6 5 4 3 2 1

CONTENTS
THE ITALIAN LANGUAGE

How to use this book 4
The sounds of Italian 7
To get you started 9

Situazione Uno: Finding the way 10
Situazione Due: Buying drinks 14
Situazione Tre: Somewhere to stay 18
Situazione Quattro: Getting information 22
Situazione Cinque: Making friends 26
Situazione Sei: Snacks and ice cream 30
Situazione Sette: Spare time 34
Situazione Otto: Getting around 38
Situazione Nove: Shopping for food 42
Situazione Dieci: Problems 46
Situazione Undici: Keeping in touch 50
Situazione Dodici: Souvenirs and gifts 54
Useful words and phrases 58

ITALY AND THE ITALIANS
Fact File 67
Daily life in Italy 70
In vacanza 87
Quiz 96

HOW TO USE THIS BOOK

WELCOME TO *DESTINATION ITALIAN!*

This book is for young people who would like to learn some Italian and find out about Italy. There are also two cassettes designed for use with the book. But don't worry if you don't have the cassettes, because the book and cassettes can also be used separately. So, whether you're in the library, on the train, in the car, or even just walking down the street, using *Destination Italian* is the perfect way to learn Italian.

The *Destination Italian* Book

The first part of the book is about the language, and the second part is about the country.
The language section contains:
- a guide to the sounds of Italian
- some Key Phrases to get you started
- twelve "situations" or **situazioni**
- a list of useful words and phrases for each situation

You can start at the first **situazione** and work through the book, or you can use them in any order you like. Each **situazione** is made up of:

Key Phrases
They will help you to understand the conversations. Try learning as many phrases as you can. When you think you know all of them, cover the English and say what the Italian

means. Then, cover each Italian phrase with a piece of paper, look at the English and say or write the Italian phrase you have covered up. Finally, ask a friend to say the English and you give the Italian. When you have done this, you could try making up different conversations with the phrases.

Conversations
Read the conversations and check that you understand them. They'll help you to say what you want in Italy.

Find Out More
Here you will find information about new words and phrases.

Over To You
This is a very important section where you will be able to check what you learned through games and short conversations, and to listen and learn to understand Italians.

Answers
Only look at the answers once you've completed all the games for each **situazione**! There is space in the book for your answers and drawings, but you could do them on paper to keep the book clean.

There is a list of additional words and phrases after the **situazioni**, on page 58. They are arranged in topics like "Shopping," "Travel," etc. There are also sections on things like numbers and colors.

All these words will help you improve your vocabulary and test yourself.

The second section of the book tells you about the Italians and the Italian way of life, and gives you information about the country itself.

The *Destination Italian* Cassettes

The cassettes start with the *Sounds of Italian* section, which gives you practice in listening to Italian and saying the sounds. Then you will be ready to work on the 12 **situazioni**.

Each **situazione** contains:

Ascolta e ripeti
This is a list of key words and phrases for you to listen to and repeat. Find the right page in the book and look at it as you listen.

Cerca la parola
You then hear some Italian words and phrases. Point to them in the book to show that you recognize them. Keep practicing until you can point to them all, as you hear them, without stopping the cassette.

Conversazioni
Listen to each conversation as you follow it in the book. Listen to the conversation again. Stop the

tape after each sentence and repeat it. Then play the conversation again and read it aloud with the tape. Finally, read the conversation aloud once more, without the cassette. When you have done this, cover up part of the conversation. Try saying the whole conversation, including the words and phrases that you have covered up.

Hai capito?
Here you can practice understanding what Italian people say by listening to conversations and checking that you understand what you hear.

Tocca a te!
Here you join in one or two conversations as if you were really in Italy and with Italian people.

THE SOUNDS OF ITALIAN

Most of the sounds of Italian are quite straightforward and once you have learned them, you can easily figure out how Italian words are pronounced when you see them for the first time.
Try saying the sounds and words on this page as you learn them.
First the vowels:
a "a" as in *father*: **banana** (*banana*)
e "e" as in *bed*: **sette** (*seven*)
i "ee" as in *meet*: **birra** (*beer*)
o "o" as in *north*: **no** (*no*)
u "oo" as in *food*: **una** (*a*)

Now the consonants:
ce "ch" as in *chess*: **cento** (*hundred*)
ci "ch" as in *chips*: **cinema** (*cinema*)
ch "k" as in *kite*: **chilo** (*kilo*)
c before any other letter is like "c" in *cat*: **capisco** (*I understand*)
ge "j" as in *jelly*: **Genova** (*Genoa*)
gi "j" as in *Jill*: **giorno** (*day*)
gh "g" as in *garden*: **spaghetti**
gli "lli" as in *million*: **biglietto** (*ticket*)
gn "ni" as in *onion*: **montagna** (*mountain*)
g before any other letter is like "g" in *gate*: **gatto** (*cat*)
h is never pronounced; just imagine it is not there: **ho sete** (*I'm thirsty*)
s has two sounds:
  "s" as in *sun*: **sono** (*I am*)
  When it is between two vowels, it sounds like "z" in *closed*: **chiuso** (*closed*)
sc when followed by "e" or "i":
  "sh" as in *show*: **scena** (*scene*); **uscita** (*exit*)
z has two sounds. Unfortunately, there is no rule for when to use each sound, so you need to learn the correct pronunciation when you learn new words.
  "ts" as in *lets*: **pizza** (*pizza*)
  "ds" as in *buds*: **zucchero** (*sugar*)
Finally, most Italian words are stressed (said more strongly) on the next-to-last syllable:
  sette   **chiuso**   **montagna**
Some words are stressed on the final vowel and these are written with an accent on the final vowel:
  città (*city*)   **caffè** (*coffee*)

8 otto

TO GET YOU STARTED

Ciao! Welcome to Italian. You might not yet know any Italian, so here is a list of useful words and phrases to get you started.

Ciao!	Hi!
	See you, Goodbye
Buongiorno	Hello
Buonasera	Good evening
Buonanotte	Good night
Arrivederci	Goodbye
Per favore	Please
Grazie	Thank you
Prego	Don't mention it/you're welcome
Sì/No	Yes/No
Scusi	Excuse me
Non capisco	I don't understand
Non lo so	I don't know
Può aiutarmi?	Can you help me?
Può scriverlo?	Can you write it down?
Può ripetere?	Can you repeat it?
Lentamente, per favore	More slowly, please
Dov'è il gabinetto?	Where is the restroom?
Mi dispiace	I'm sorry
Mi sono perso(a)	I'm lost
Signore	Mr. (Sir)
Signora	Mrs. (Sir)
Signorina	Miss
e/o	and/or
anche	also

SITUAZIONE UNO

FINDING THE WAY

When you arrive in a town, you will probably need to ask for directions on how to get downtown, **il centro**, and to the tourist office, **l'ufficio turistico**. Here are some useful phrases to help you ask for and understand directions.

KEY PHRASES

Scusi, dov'è . . .?	Excuse me, where is . . .?
Il campeggio	The campsite
L'ufficio postale	The post office
La spiaggia	The beach
Prenda la prima strada a destra	Take the first street on the right
Prenda la seconda strada a sinistra	Take the second street on the left
Vada sempre dritto	Go straight ahead
Giri a sinistra	Turn left
Giri a destra	Turn right
È lontano?	Is it far?
No, è vicino al duomo	No, it is near the cathedral

Jane and Simon have just arrived in an Italian town. Where does Jane want to go?

Where does Simon want to go to?

Find Out More

1. Here are the names of more places that you might want to find. Can you guess what they are?

| IL RISTORANTE | LA PIZZERIA |

| LA STAZIONE | LA BANCA | LA FARMACIA |

2. "The" is **il**, **la**, **l'**, or **lo**. When you learn new words, you should also learn the word for "the":

il duomo   *la* spiaggia
*l'*ufficio turistico   *lo* stadio

It is important to understand why these are different. In Italian all nouns or "things" are either masculine (m) **il duomo**, or feminine (f) **la spiaggia**. Most masculine nouns end in "o" and most feminine nouns end in "a." Use **il** to mean "the" for most masculine nouns, but **l'** for any beginning with a vowel (a,e,i,o,u), e.g., **l'ufficio turistico** and **lo** for any beginning with a "z" e.g., **zucchero** (sugar) or "s" followed by another consonant e.g., **lo stadio**. However, use **la** for all feminine nouns except those beginning with a vowel when you also use **l'** e.g., **l'aranciata**.

3. Here are some more directions:

Attraversi la strada   Cross the road
Attraversi il ponte   Cross the bridge
Attraversi la piazza   Cross the square
Al semaforo   To the traffic lights
All'incrocio   To the intersection

4. **È lontano** (?) means *It is far* or *Is it far?* To say it is not far, simply put **non** in front of the phrase: **Non è lontano**.

Over To You

1. Ask the way to these different places. Example: **Scusi, dov'è il duomo?**

_____ ? _____ ? _____ ?

2. Fill in the missing vowels (*a, e, i, o, u*) to complete these phrases.
(a) Sc_s_, d_v'_ l'_ff_c_ _ p_st_l_?
(b) P_ _ r_p_t_r_, p_r f_v_r_?
(c) _ l_nt_n_? (d) Gr_z_ _

3. Now, using the phrases from question 2, complete this conversation:

You:

_____

Passer-by: **Prenda la prima strada a sinistra, poi vada sempre dritto, al semaforo.**
You:

_____

Passer-by: **Sì, certo. Prenda la prima a sinistra, vada sempre dritto, al semaforo.**
You:

_____

Passer-by: **No, non è lontano.**
You:

_____

Passer-by: **Prego.**

ANSWERS
Jane asks the way to the tourist office. Simon asks for the campsite.
OVER TO YOU
1. Scusi, dov'è il campeggio? Scusi, dov'è l'ufficio turistico? Scusi, dov'è la stazione?
2. Scusi, dov'è l'ufficio postale? Può ripetere, per favore? È lontano? Grazie

SITUAZIONE TRE

BUYING DRINKS

In an Italian cafe, **un bar**, you can buy many different soft drinks, hot and cold drinks as well as alcoholic drinks. Why not try **una granita** (*a crushed ice drink*) or **una spremuta** (*fresh fruit juice*)?

KEY PHRASES

Mi dica	What would you like?
Vorrei . . .	I would like
Un caffè	A coffee
Un caffelatte	A coffee with milk
Un cappuccino	A coffee with frothy milk
Un succo di frutta	A fruit juice
Un succo d'arancia	An orange juice
Un'aranciata	An orangeade
Ho sete	I'm thirsty
Quant'è?	How much is it?
Millecinquecento lire	1,500 lire
Duemila lire/seimila lire	2,000 lire/6,000 lire

Jane is with her friends Daria and Simon in a cafe. Do you like the same drinks as they do?

- Mi dica.
- Un caffelatte . . .
- Un caffelatte, per favore.
- Vorrei un'aranciata, per favore.
- Un caffelatte e un' aranciata.

Simon is also thirsty.

- Un succo d'arancia?
- Ho sete. Un succo di frutta, per favore.
- Sì. Quant'è?
- Duemila lire.

Find Out More

1. "A" is **un**, **una**, **un'**, or **uno**. When you learn new words, you should also learn the word for "a:"
un cappuccino **un'aranciata** **una spremuta**
uno scontrino (a receipt)
Remember that in Italian all nouns are either masculine or feminine. Use **un** to mean "a" for most masculine nouns, with **uno** for any beginning with a "z" e.g., **zucchero** or "s" plus another consonant e.g., **scontrino**. Use **una** as "a" for all feminine nouns, except those beginning with a vowel when you use **un'** e.g., **un'aranciata**.
2. If you ask for **un caffè**, you will be given **un espresso**, a small cup of strong black coffee. If you want milk in it, ask for **un caffelatte** or **un cappuccino**.
3. Here are a few more drinks you may like to have:
una cioccolata calda *(hot chocolate)*
un tè al limone *(tea with lemon)*
un tè al latte *(tea with milk)*
4. When you order, the waiter may respond with **Subito** *(immediately)*. When he brings your drinks, he may say **Ecco** (*Here you are*) as he puts them on the table. For more information on cafes and bars, see page 79.
5. For more information on numbers and prices, see pages 61 and 62.

Over To You

1. Find the seven drinks entangled in this word snake. Write them out. Practice asking for them.
Example: **Vorrei una spremuta, per favore.**
SPREMUTACAFFETEARANCIATA
CAFFELATTECIOCCOLATACAP
PUCCINO _____ _____ _____

_____ _____ _____ _____

2. You go to a *cafe*. Write in the spaces what you would say in Italian.
Waiter: **Buongiorno. Mi dica.**
You: Ask for a coffee with milk and an orange juice.

_____

Waiter: **Subito.**
You: Ask how much it is.

_____

Waiter: **Quattromila lire.**

3. Order drinks for your friends who don't speak Italian.
Example: Tea with milk, please.
Vorrei un tè al latte, per favore.
Er . . . hot chocolate, please.
I'll have a coffee.
And I'll have an orangeade.

ANSWERS

1. Spremuta; caffè; tè; aranciata; caffellatte; cioccolata; cappuccino.
2. Vorrei una spremuta (un caffè) un tè; un'aranciata; un caffellatte; una cioccolata, un cappuccino) per favore. Un caffellatte e un succo d'arancia, per favore; Quant'è?
3. Vorrei una cioccolata calda, per favore; Un caffè, per favore; E un'aranciata.

SITUAZIONE DUE

SOMEWHERE TO STAY

When you go to Italy, you may stay in **un albergo** (*a hotel*), with a family, or in **un ostello della gioventù** (*a youth hostel*). However, if you are traveling around, you may prefer to **fare il campeggio** (*go camping*).

KEY PHRASES

Buonasera.	Good evening.
C'è ancora posto per stasera?	Do you have a room for tonight?
Per quante persone?	For how many people?
Per due persone	For two people
C'è posto per una tenda?	Do you have room for a tent?
Per quanto tempo?	For how long?
Per una settimana/tre notti	For one week/three nights
Dov'è lo spaccio?	Where is the store?
C'è un ristorante?	Is there a restaurant?
A che ora si apre/si chiude?	What time does it open/close?
Alle otto	At eight o'clock
Dove sono le docce?	Where are the showers?
Sono vicino al ristorante	They are near the restaurant

Jane and Simon arrive at a campsite. How long do they want to stay?

Buonasera, signora. C'è ancora posto per stasera?

Per quante persone?

Per due persone e due tende.

E per quanto tempo?

Per quattro notti.

What does Jane want to know?

Scusi, signora, dove sono le docce?

Sono vicino al ristorante.

E c'è uno spaccio?

Sì . . . ma si chiude alle otto.

Grazie, signora.

diciannove 19

Find Out More

1. **C'è** means *There is.* **C'è posto?** *Is there any room?* **C'è un ristorante?** *Is there a restaurant?* **Ci sono** means *There are.* **Ci sono due ristoranti** *There are two restaurants.*
2. You ask **C'è posto?** when looking for a place at **un ostello della gioventù** (*a youth hostel*). However, in a hotel, you ask for a room: **Ha una camera?** (*Do you have a room?*).
3. A campsite for a tent or a caravan is **una piazzuola**. You may be given a number to help you find your campsite. **Piazzuola numero diciotto**. For more information on numbers, see page 61.
4. A campsite shop is **uno spaccio**. Otherwise, a shop is **un negozio**. For more information on opening times, see page 70.

Over To You

1. When you register, the receptionist gives you **un modulo** (a form) to complete. Can you figure out what information you must give?

CAMPEGGIO DEL LAGO			
COGNOME	*WALKER*	**NAZIONALITÀ**	*AMERICANO*
NOME	*DANIEL*	**DATA DI ARRIVO**	*15/7/95*
INDIRIZZO	*1413 FULLERTON*	**NUMERO DI PASSAPORTO**	
	CHICAGO, ILLINOIS 60614		*P138745D*
	GLI STATI UNITI	**FIRMA**	*Daniel Walker*

2. To check you can, fill in this form with your personal details.

CAMPEGGIO DEL LAGO	
COGNOME _____	NAZIONALITÀ _____
NOME _____	DATA DI ARRIVO _____
INDIRIZZO	NUMERO DI PASSAPORTO _____
	FIRMA

3. Find and circle in this grid, six words connected with staying at a campsite. Then use four of the words to complete the conversation.

```
S T X Y Q O S
P E R S O N E
A N O T T I R
C D E I B L V
C A P O R C I
I V R E M S Z
O T S C U S I
```

_____ , signora. C'è ancora posto per stasera?
Per quante persone?
Per due _____ e per una _____ .
E per quanto tempo?
Per quattro _____ .
Sì, c'è posto. Piazzuola numero dieci.

ANSWERS

Jane and Simon want to stay for four nights. Jane wants to know where the showers are and whether there's a store on the campsite.

OVER TO YOU

2. To fill in the form, you should give your name (family name and first name); address; nationality; date of arrival; passport number and then sign it.

3. Scusi, signora. C'è ancora posto per stasera?
Per quante persone?
Per due persone e per una tenda.
E per quanto tempo?
Per quattro notti.
Sì, c'è posto. Piazzuola numero dieci.

ventuno 21

SITUAZIONE QUATTRO

GETTING INFORMATION

The best place to get information, as well as maps and leaflets on local events, is **l'ufficio turistico** (*the tourist office*). Here are some useful phrases to help you.

KEY PHRASES

Ha una pianta della città?	Do you have a map of the city?
Vorrei un dépliant della regione	I would like a pamphlet on the region
Sì . . . in inglese o in italiano?	Yes . . . in English or in Italian?
Ha delle informazioni sulle gite turistiche?	Do you have any information on trips?
Ecco un dépliant	Here is a leaflet.
Mi può dare una lista dei campeggi?	Can you give me a list of campsites?
Sì, certo	Yes, of course
Desidera altro?	Would you like anything else?
Che cosa c'è da fare?	What is there to do?
Dunque, c'è una piscina	Well, there is a swimming pool
Si può visitare i monumenti/andare in spiaggia	You can visit the monuments/go to the beach

Jane and Simon are finding out some information so that they can plan a few activities.

Buongiorno.

Ha una pianta della regione, per favore?

Sì, certo. Ecco. Desidera altro?

Sì, vorrei anche delle informazioni sulle gite turistiche.

Would you be interested in any of the activities that are mentioned?

Che cosa c'è da fare?

Mi può dare un dépliant della città?

Dunque, si può visitare i monumenti o si può andare in spiaggia. C'è anche una piscina.

Sì . . . in inglese o in italiano?

In italiano.

Find Out More

1. When finding out what is available, you can ask **Ha . . .?** (*Do you have . . .?*) followed by what it is you are asking for:
Ha una pianta della regione?
2. To ask for something, you can begin with **Vorrei . . .** (*I would like . . .*) or **Mi può dare?** (*Can you give me . . .?*).
Vorrei una lista degli alberghi.
Mi può dare una lista dei campeggi?
3. When talking about more than one thing, the word for "the" changes. The word ending for the thing also changes. As a general rule, words that end in **-a** in the singular, end in **-e** in the plural. Words that end in **-o** in the singular end in **-i** in the plural.

singular	plural	singular	plural
la pianta	*le* piante	*l'*albergo	*gli* alberghi
Ecco le piante		Mi piacciono gli alberghi italiani	
il museo	*i* musei	*lo* scontrino	*gli* scontrini

Si può visitare i musei.   Ecco gli scontrini.

Over To You

1. Can you match the following questions and answers?
(1) **Ha un dépliant della città?**
(2) **Che cosa c'è da fare?**

(a) **In inglese, per favore.**
(b) **Sì . . . ecco un dépliant.**

(3) **Desidera altro?** (c) **Sì, certo. Ecco.**
(4) **In inglese o in italiano?** (d) **Sì, vorrei anche una pianta della regione.**
(5) **Ha delle informazioni sulla festa?** (e) **Si può visitare la cattedrale ed i monumenti.**

2. Look carefully at these pictures. Can you use each one in a different sentence or question to complete the conversation?

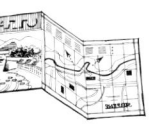

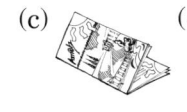

(a) (c) (d) (b)

SITUAZIONE CINQUE

MAKING FRIENDS

Traveling in Italy will give you a really good opportunity to meet young Italians and make friends with them. This will help you to learn to speak their language. Here are some useful phrases to get you started.

KEY PHRASES

Sei inglese?	Are you English?
Sono scozzese	I am Scottish
Di dove sei?	Where are you from?
Sono di (Londra)	I'm from (London)
Come ti chiami?	What is your name?
Mi chiamo . . .	My name is . . .
Quanti anni hai?	How old are you?
Ho tredici anni	I'm thirteen
E tu?	And you?
Come va?	How are you?
Va bene, grazie	Fine, thank you
Sei in vacanza?	Are you on vacation?

Jane and Simon meet up with some young Italians at the swimming pool.

Sei inglese?

Sì, sono di Londra. E tu?

Sono italiano. Mi chiamo Roberto. E tu?

Mi chiamo Jane.

What are they talking about?

E tu, come ti chiami?

Giulia. Sei inglese?

Sì, mi chiamo Simon. Sono in vacanza.

Come va?

Bene, grazie.

Find Out More

1. It is important to use the correct form when talking to people in Italian. When greeting an adult you don't know every well, you say **Buongiorno**. When speaking to someone of your own age, you can say **Ciao**! Similarly, when asking for someone's name, you ask **Come si chiama**? when talking to an adult you don't know well and **Come ti chiami**? when talking to someone of your own age.

2. **Americano/a** means American, and **inglese** means English. Other nationalities you may find useful to know are **canadese** (*Canadian*), **irlandese** (*Irish*), **scozzese** (*Scottish*), **australiano** (*Australian*). For more information on countries and nationalities, see pages 62 and 63.

3. For more information on numbers, see page 61.

Over To You

1. Can you figure out what these questions are?

(a) Come ti chiami ? (b) Quanti anni hai ?
(c) Di dove sei ? (d) Sei in vacanza ?

2. Now answer the questions!

(a) _____

(b) _____

(c) _____

(d) _____

3. You meet a young Italian girl at the campsite shop and would like to get to know her. Can you complete this dialogue?

Lorella: **Ciao! Sei inglese?**
You: Tell her your nationality.

Lorella: **Di sove sei?**
You: Tell her where you come from and ask her where she comes from.

Lorella: **Sono di Milano. Mi chiamo Lorella. E tu?**
You: Tell her your name and ask her if she is on vacation here.

Lorella: **Sì ...**

ANSWERS

They are all introducing themselves, and finding out about each other.

OVER TO YOU

1. (a) Come ti chiami? (b) Quanti anni hai? (c) Di dove sei? (d) Sei in vacanza?

SITUAZIONE SEI

SNACKS AND ICE CREAM

When you need a break from sightseeing and tours and are also in need of something to eat, you will be able to find many places where you can stop and buy a snack. Here are some phrases to help you get what you want to eat.

KEY PHRASES

Un panino, per favore	A sandwich, please
Vorrei un tramezzino al formaggio, per favore	I would like a cheese sandwich, please
Un toast	A toasted sandwich
Un panino al prosciutto	A ham sandwich
Mi dà un po' di pizza	Can I have a slice of pizza?
Vorrei un gelato, per favore	I would like an ice cream, please
Grande o piccolo?	Large or small?
Cosa preferisce?	What would you like?
Fragola / nocciola / crema / cioccolato	Strawberry / hazelnut / vanilla / chocolate
Un po' di questo, per favore	Some of this one, please
Quanto costa?	How much is it?
Settemila lire	7,000 lire

While sightseeing, Jane and Simon decide to stop and eat. What does Jane order?

Un panino al prosciutto, al formaggio . . . ?

Un panino e un toast, per favore.

Al prosciutto. Quanto costa?

Allora, un panino e un toast . . . settemila lire.

What does Simon want to eat?

Vorrei un gelato, per favore.

Sì, certo . . . grande o piccolo?

Grande.

Cosa preferisce?

Fragola, crema e un po' di questo, per favore.

Find Out More

1. Cafés and bars sell **panini** (*sandwiches*) and **tramezzini** (*tea sandwiches*). Some also sell ice cream. For a wider choice, head for **una paninoteca** (*sandwich shop*). For ice cream, look for **una gelateria**.
2. When buying ice cream, you can choose either **un cono** (*a cone*) or **una coppa** (*a cup*). Other flavors you could try are **limone** (*lemon*), **caffè** (*coffee*), **banana** (*banana*), **albicocca** (*apricot*), or **pistacchio** (*pistachio*). If you would like an ice cream **con pana**, with whipped cream on it, you could say, for example: **Mi dà un gelato al cioccolato con panna**.
3. If you are not sure how to ask for a particular flavor, simply point and say **un po' di questo, per favore** (*some of this, please*). If you are buying **pizza al taglio** (*a slice of pizza*), you can point and ask for **un po' di questa** (*a bit of this one*).

Over To You

1. How would you ask for each of these items?

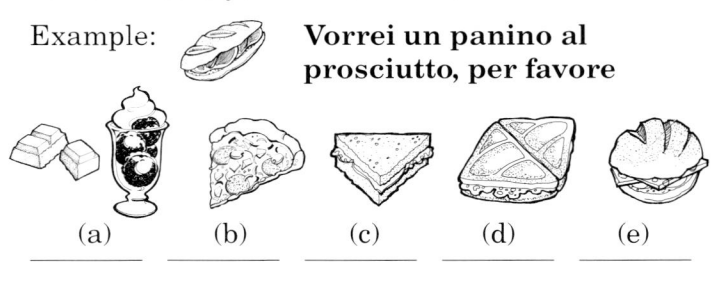

Example: **Vorrei un panino al prosciutto, per favore**

(a)   (b)   (c)   (d)   (e)

2. Can you complete this list of flavors at the **gelateria**?

un gelato al cioccolato

_____   _____

_____   _____

3. You're hungry. Complete the conversation to make sure you get something to eat.

Waiter: **Buongiorno. Mi dica!**
You: Say you would like a sandwich.

_____

Waiter: **Al prosciutto . . . al formaggio . . .?**
You: Say you would like a cheese sandwich.

_____

Waiter: **Ecco.**
You: Say you would also like an ice cream.

_____

Waiter: **Cosa preferisce?**
You: Tell him the flavors that you like!

_____

ANSWERS

Jane orders a ham sandwich and toast, while Simon wants a large ice cream.

OVER TO YOU
1. Vorrei un gelato al cioccolato; Mi dà un po' di pizza; Vorrei un tramezzino, per favore; Mi dà un toast; Vorrei un panino al formaggio.
2. limone; fragola; nocciola; caffè; albicocca; banana.

trentatre 33

SITUAZIONE SETTE

SPARE TIME

When you are on vacation, it is great to be able to go out and do things. It is also useful to be able to say what you like doing so that you can make plans for your spare time. Here are some useful phrases to get you started.

KEY PHRASES

Che cosa facciamo stasera/domani?	What shall we do this evening/tomorrow?
Ti piacerebbe andare al cinema/a teatro/in pizzeria?	Would you like to go to the movies/to the theater/to a pizzeria?
Sì, molto	Yes, I would
Non molto. Mi dispiace	Not really. I'm sorry
Che cosa danno al cinema?	What's playing at the movies?
C'è un bel film	There is a good film
Perfetto!	Great!
Facciamo un giro in centro?	Shall we go downtown?
Andiamo in piscina	Let's go to the swimming pool.
A che ora?	At what time?
Alle nove (alle dieci).	At 9 (10 o'clock)
D'accordo	OK

Jane and Simon are with Roberto and Giulia.
They are deciding what they are going to do.

Ti piacerebbe andare al cinema?

Che cosa facciamo stasera?

Sì, molto. Che cosa danno?

C'è un bel film all'Astra.

Perfetto!

Would you be interested in going with them?

E che cosa facciamo domani?

Mi piacerebbe fare un giro in centro.

A che ora?

Alle dieci?

Sì, d'accordo.

Find Out More

1. You may be asked what you would like to do: **stamattina** (*this morning*); **stasera** (*this evening*); **oggi pomeriggio** (*this afternoon*); or **domani** (*tomorrow*). For example: **Ti piacerebbe andare in discoteca stasera?** (*Would you like to go to the disco tonight?*)
2. **Andiamo** can mean: *We are going* or *Let's go* or even *Shall we go?*: **Andiamo a Firenze!** Let's go to Florence!
3. If you really like a suggestion, you can reply **Volentieri** (*with pleasure*). However, if you would rather do something else, you could say **Preferirei . . .** (*I would rather . . .*). **Preferirei andare in piscina** (*I would rather go to the swimming pool*).
4. A film on television or at the movie theater is **un film**. Film that you put in your camera is **una pellicola**.

Over To You

1. Can you complete these phrases by filling in the missing vowels?

(a) s__, v__l__nt__r__.   (b) __ ch__ __r__?

(c) Ch__ c__s__ f__cc__ __m__ st__s__r__?

(d) __ll__ n__v__.

(e) F__cc__ __m__ __n g__r__?

2. Now rearrange the phrases to make a sensible dialogue.

3. Starting with the letter A, can you figure out where Luisa wants to go?

4. What would you answer?

ANSWERS

1. Che cosa facciamo stasera? (c)
Facciamo un giro? (e)
A che ora? (b)
Sì, volentieri. (a)
Alle nove. (d)

3. Luisa says:
Andiamo in piscina? Shall we go to the swimming pool?

SITUAZIONE OTTO

GETTING AROUND

Getting around Italy is easy. You can take **l' autobus** (*the bus*), or possibly **un tram** (*a tram*), if you are not going too far. For a longer journey, you can take **un pullman** (*a coach*) or **un treno** (*a train*). In Milan or Rome you can also take **la Metropolitana** (*the subway*). Here are some key phrases to help you get around.

KEY PHRASES

Mi dà un biglietto per l'autobus?	Can I have a ticket for the bus?
Quant'è?	How much is it?
Duemilaquattrocento lire (seimila lire)	2,400 lire (6,000) lire
L'autobus per la stazione / la piscina / il campeggio, per favore	The bus for the station / swimming pool / campsite, please
Deve prendere il numero undici	You need to catch the number 11
Due biglietti per Firenze, per favore	Two tickets for Florence, please
Andata e ritorno	Round-trip
Solo andata	One-way
A che ora parte / arriva?	What time does it leave / arrive?
Da che binario parte?	From what platform does it leave?
Dal binario nove	From platform 9

Jane and Simon decide to go to Venice for the day. How do they get to the train station?

Mi dà due biglietti per l'autobus, per favore.

Ecco ... duemilaquattrocento.

L'autobus per la stazione, per favore?

Per la stazione? Deve prendere il numero undici.

Grazie.

What do they ask for at the station?

Due biglietti per Venezia, per favore.

Solo andata?

No, andata e ritorno. Da che binario parte?

Dal binario nove.

Grazie.

Find Out More

1. When using buses in towns or cities, you have to buy your ticket before you board. There is a flat rate and **biglietti** (*tickets*) can be bought from **un'edicola** (*a newspaper stand*) or where you see the **Tabacchi** sign. You can also buy a block of ten tickets, **un blocchetto**, which is cheaper. You get on the bus by the door marked **Entrata** and leave by the door marked **Uscita**.
For more information on travel by bus, see page 77.

2. When looking at **l'orario** (*the schedule*) for information, you will find the times of **Partenze** (*departures)* and **Arrivi** (*arrivals*). For more information on travel by train, see page 76.

3. **Un biglietto** is any type of a ticket. For example, to buy a ticket for the movies, you could ask: **Due biglietti per Hook: Capitan Uncino, per favore**. Or you could simply state the number: **Due per Hook, per favore.**

Over To You

1. In each jumble of letters below, is the name of an Italian city. Can you figure out each name? Write them out. You may need an atlas to help you.

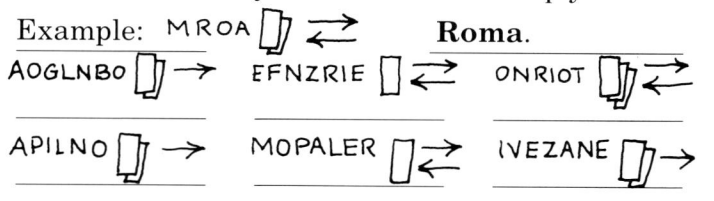

Example: MROA ⇄ **Roma**.

AOGLNBO →

EFNZRIE ⇄

ONRIOT ⇄

APILNO →

MOPALER ⇄

IVEZANE →

2. Look at the number of tickets next to each city. How would you ask for the tickets you need?

Example: MROA 🎫 ⇄ **Due biglietti per Roma, andata e ritorno, per favore**.

3. Can you figure out what Stefano is asking?

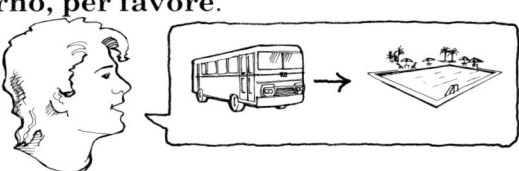

You can make up your own picture sentences to help you learn. Try it on some of the key phrases from page 38.

4. Complete this conversation:

You: Ask for a book of ten bus tickets.

SITUAZIONE NOVE

SHOPPING FOR FOOD

If you are going out for the day, it is a good idea to take a picnic. This will give you an excuse to go shopping for food while in Italy, which is great fun and very interesting. Here are some phrases to help you buy the things you need.

KEY PHRASES

Buongiorno. Mi dica	Good morning. Can I help you?
Otto panini, per favore	Eight sandwiches, please
Vuole altro?	Anything else?
Mi dà mezzo chilo di pomodori	Give me 500 grams of tomatoes
Un chilo di mele / pesche	A kilo of apples / peaches
Vorrei anche un po' d'uva	I would also like some grapes
Va bene così?	Is that enough?
Sì, va bene, grazie	Yes, that's fine, thank you
Un po' di più/meno	A little bit more/less
Mi dà tre etti di formaggio	Give me 300 grams of cheese
Vorrei quattro fette di prosciutto, per favore	I would like four slices of ham, please
Mi dà una bottiglia d'acqua minerale	Give me a bottle of mineral water

Jane and Simon are with Roberto and Giulia.
They are in the **alimentari**.

> **Quattro fette di prosciutto e tre etti di formaggio, per favore.**
>
> Vuole altro?
>
> Otto panini.
>
> Ecco... vuole altro?
>
> Sì... vorrei anche una bottiglia d'acqua.

What do they buy for their picnic?

> Mi dà mezzo chilo di pomodori e un chilo di pesche, per favore.
>
> Vuole altro?
>
> Sì... un po' d'uva, per favore.
>
> Va bene così?
>
> Un po' di più, per favore.

Find Out More

1. You will probably be able to get nearly every kind of food you need in **un alimentari** (*a general store*). Many Italian towns have **un mercato** (*a market*) where you can buy fruit and vegetables, and you can buy many different types of **pane** (*bread*) at **una panetteria** (*a bakery*). For delicious **paste** (*pastries and cakes*) look for **una pasticceria**.
2. **Un chilo** is just over two pounds in weight. For half that amount, ask for **mezzo chilo** or **cinquencento grammi**. 100 grams is **un etto**.
3. You will find a wide selection of fruit at a market stall: **delle mele** (*apples*), **delle fragole** (*strawberries*), **delle albicocche** (*apricots*), **delle banane** (*bananas*). For more information on food and drink, see page 58.
4. To buy things in Italy, you will need some **lire**. For more information on money—notes and coins—see page 68. Price labels are usually written: L 3500.

Over To You

1. Can you match up the two halves of these phrases?
   (1) **mezzo chilo**   (a) **di prosciutto**
   (2) **un chilo**   (b) **di formaggio**
   (3) **una bottiglia**   (c) **di pomodori**
   (4) **un po'**   (d) **di mele**
   (5) **tre fette**   (e) **d'acqua minerale**

2. Each of the phrases in question 1 is represented in this conversation by a picture. Can you complete the conversation?

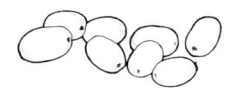

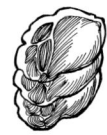

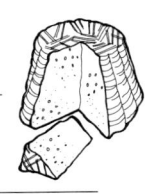

SITUAZIONE DIECI

PROBLEMS

Although you will probably have a great time on vacation, sometimes things can go wrong. However, the more prepared you are, the less likely you are to worry and panic. So here are some useful phrases to help you deal with problems.

KEY PHRASES

Che cosa è successo?	What has happened?
Ho perso la mia borsa / il mio zaino / il mio passaporto / il mio portafoglio	I have lost by bag / my backpack / my passport / my wallet
Andiamo all'Ufficio Oggetti Smarriti	Let's go to the Lost and Found office
Non preoccuparti!	Don't worry!
Dove l'hai perso?	Where did you lose it?
Vicino al ristorante / alla stazione / sull'autobus / in spiaggia	Near the restaurant / the station / on the bus / on the beach
Com'è?	What is it like?
È grande / piccolo / nero / bianco / rosso	It is big / small / black / white / red
È questo / questa?	Is it this one?
Sì, è il mio / la mia	Yes, it's mine
Che fortuna!	What a relief!

Simon has lost his wallet. Where exactly does he think he lost it?

Che cosa è successo?

Ho perso il mio portafoglio.

Dove l'hai perso?

Sull'autobus.

Non preoccuparti... andiamo all'Ufficio Oggetti Smarriti.

What does his wallet look like?

Com'è il portafoglio?

È piccolo e nero.

È questo?

Che fortuna! Sì, è il mio... grazie.

Prego.

Find Out More

1. If you lose your passport or other valuables, or if they are stolen, you should go to the **Questura** (*police station*) as it will be necessary to **fare una denuncia** (*make a statement*).
2. As you have seen, **Non preoccuparti!** means *Don't worry!*
3. è means *it is*: **è rosso**, *it is red*.
Without an accent, **e** means *and*.
4. If you are describing a feminine noun, for example, **una borsa**, the adjective ending usually changes to **a: la mia borsa è rossa**. However, if an adjective ends in **e**, it stays the same. **Il mio zaino è grande; La mia borsa è grande**.

Over To You

1. Follow the lines and unscramble the words to find out what each person would reply to the question: Che cosa è successo?

Lorella: **Ho perso il mio** — (nzoia)

Chiara: **Ho perso la mia** — (prspoastoa)

Fabrizio: **Ho perso il mio** — (srbao)

Gianni: **Ho perso il mio** — (ofgiptaloor)

2. Which is the odd-one-out in each column?

rosso	**zaino**	**bianco**
grande	**borsa**	**grande**
nero	**passaporto**	**piccolo**
bianco	**portafoglio**	

3. You are in the Lost and Found office. Can you complete the dialogue?

You: Say you have lost your wallet.

SITUAZIONE UNDICI

KEEPING IN TOUCH

You will probably want to send postcards to your family and friends to tell them what a great time you are having. Keeping in touch by mail or by phone is very straightforward. Here are some key phrases to help you get started.

KEY PHRASES

Mi dà tre francobolli per l'Inghilterra	Give me three stamps for England
Per cartoline o per lettere?	For postcards or letters?
Per cartoline	For postcards
Settecento lire	700 lire
Sono duemilacento lire	That is 2,100 lire
Quanto costano le cartoline, per favore	How much are the postcards, please?
Costano trecento lire	They cost 300 lire
Va bene . . . ne prendo tre	Very well . . . I'll have three of them
Vorrei anche una carta telefonica	I would also like a phone card
Da cinquemila o da diecimila lire?	5,000 or 10,000 lire?
Da cinquemila	5,000
Tenga. Grazie	Here you are. Thank you

Jane and Simon are catching up on their correspondence.

> **Buongiorno. Mi dà tre francobolli per l'Inghilterra, per cartoline.**

> **Ecco. Sono duemilacento lire.**

> **Quanto costano le cartoline?**

> **Costano trecento lire.**

> **Va bene... ne prendo quattro.**

How much money do they spend in total?

> **Vorrei una carta telefonica, per favore.**

> **Da cinquemila o da diecimila lire?**

> **Da diecimila.**

> **Ecco.**

> **Tenga. Grazie.**

Find Out More

1. Stamps, postcards, and phone cards can all be bought at **tabaccheria**, where you see this sign:

Mail boxes are yellow or red and labeled **Poste**. For more information on postal services, see pages 73 and 74.

2. Phone cards (**carte telefoniche** or **schede telefoniche**) are very practical. However, you can also use coin phone boxes. These take **monete** *(coins)* of 100 or 200 lire. They also take **gettoni** *(tokens)*, which can also be purchased at a tabaccheria. To ask for tokens for the phone, you can simply ask **Avete dei gettoni?** The Italian for small change is **spiccioli**. For more information on using phones in Italy, see page 74.

3. The names of countries are preceded by **la, l', il,** or **gli: gli Stati Uniti; l'Inghilterra; la Scozia; l'Irlanda; il Galles; l'Australia; la Francia**. To buy a stamp for Scotland, you would say, for example: **Mi dà un francobollo per la Scozia, per favore.**

For more information on names of countries in Italian, see pages 62 and 63.

Over To You

1. Read these sentences carefully. Which would you be likely to hear and which would you be likely to say?

(a) **Mi dà tre francobolli per gli Stati Uniti.**
(b) **Sono duemilacento lire.**
(c) **Da cinquemila o da diecimila?**
(d) **Per cartoline.**
(e) **Da diecimila.**
(f) **Per lettere o per cartoline?**
(g) **Vorrei anche una carta telefonica.**

2. Now put the phrases in question 1 in order to make a sensible conversation. Make it polite. Add **Buongiorno** at the beginning and don't forget to say "Thank you" at the end!

3. Now complete this conversation:

SITUAZIONE DODICI

SOUVENIRS AND GIFTS

It can be great fun looking for the ideal present for your family and friends or for yourself. In Italy you will be able to choose from a wide range of small boutiques, some department stores, or the local **mercato** *(market)*. Here are some key phrases to help you buy the perfect present.

KEY PHRASES

Sto cercando un regalo per un'amica	I am looking for a present for a friend
Abbiamo delle T-shirt (degli orecchini / delle sciarpe)	We have T-shirts (earrings / scarves)
Quanto costano questi orecchini?	How much are these earrings?
Quanto costa questo portafoglio?	How much is this wallet?
Costa quarantamila lire / Costano venticinquemila lire	It costs 40,000 lire / They cost 25,000 lire
Posso provare questa giacca?	Can I try on this jacket?
Le piace?	Do you like it?
È molto bello / bella	It is nice (lovely)
Mi dispiace	I'm sorry
È troppo cara	It is too expensive
Sono troppo cari/care	They are too expensive
Mi piace. Prendo questo / questa.	I like it. I'll take this one

Jane and Simon are shopping with Roberto and Giulia. Who is Jane shopping for?

Sto cercando un regalo per un'amica.

Allora... abbiamo degli orecchini, delle sciarpe.

Quanto costano questi orecchini?

Costano venticinquemila lire.

Mi dispiace. Sono troppo cari.

Is Simon pleased with his purchase?

Posso provare questa giacca?

Sì... Le piace?

Sì, è molto bella. Quanto costa?

Quarantamila lire.

Mi piace... prendo questa.

Find Out More

1. When talking about a male friend, you say **un amico: Sto cercando un regalo per un amico**. When talking about a female friend, you say **un'amica**.
2. When asking the price of one item, you ask **Quanto costa? Quanto costa questa t-shirt?** However, when asking the price of more than one item, you ask **Quanto costano? Quanto costano questi orecchini?** You can also say **Quant'è?** (*How much is it?*)
2. Similarly, when saying that you like a single item, you say **Mi piace: Mi piace questa maglia**. When saying that you like more than one item, you say **Mi piacciono: Mi piacciono queste sciarpe**.
3. If you ask to try an item of clothing, the assistant will ask **Che taglia?** (*What size?*) For information on Italian clothes sizes, see page 64.
4. **Mi piace** means *I like*. **Non mi piace** means *I don't like*: **Non mi piacciono questi orecchini**.

Over To You

1. How would you ask how much each of these items costs?

Example: **Quanto costa questo portafoglio?**

2. Look carefully at the symbols. What would you reply to the question: **Le piace?**

Example: Sì, mi piace.

_____

_____

_____

3. To show that you know how to buy souvenirs and gifts in Italy, complete this dialogue.

USEFUL WORDS AND PHRASES

In this section you'll find additional words and phrases. These are related to the twelve **situazoni** and are listed by theme: places, food and drink, accommodation, relatives and friends, spare time, travel and transportation, shopping, health. These are followed by a list of words relating to: numbers, prices, money, days of the week and months of the year, countries and nationalities, time, weather, colors, and clothing sizes. You will also find some useful acronyms.

PLACES
la banca	bank
la farmacia	pharmacy
il mercato	market
il museo	museum
l'ospedale	hospital
la questura	police station
il supermercato	supermarket

FOOD AND DRINK
la (prima) colazione	breakfast
il pranzo	lunch
la cena	dinner
una birra	beer
una coca cola	coca cola
un succo di pompelmo	grapefruit juice
un succo d'arancia	orange juice
la minestra	soup
della pastasciutta	pasta
della carne	meat
il pollo	chicken
il pesce	fish
l'insalata	salad
della verdura	vegetables
delle patate fritte	french fries
degli zucchini	zucchini
dei carciofi	artichokes
i pomodori	tomatoes
i piselli	peas
un bicchiere (di)	a glass (of)

una tazza (di)	a cup (of)
ho fame	I'm hungry
ho sete	I'm thirsty

ACCOMMODATION

un albergo	a hotel
un campeggio	a campsite
un ostello della gioventù	a youth hostel
una camera	a room
una piazzuola	a campsite
la chiave	the key
ho prenotato	I have reserved
singola	single
doppia	double
il bagno	bathroom
la doccia	shower
il gabinetto	restroom
pensione completa	full board
mezza pensione	half board
completo	full
una tessera	a membership card
non funziona	it doesn't work

RELATIVES AND FRIENDS

i genitori	parents
un fratello	brother
una sorella	sister
un padre	father
una madre	mother
uno zio	uncle
una zia	aunt
un cugino	(male) cousin
una cugina	(female) cousin
una famiglia	family
un amico	(male) friend
un'amica	(female) friend

SPARE TIME

Ti piace . . .?	Do you like . . .?
la musica	music
lo sport	sport
il calcio	football
il nuoto	swimming
giocare	to play (a game)

cinquantanove 59

suonare	to play (a musical instrument)
la chitarra	guitar
leggere	to read
guardare	to watch
uno spettacolo	a show

TRAVEL AND TRANSPORTATION

un viaggio	a journey
una macchina	a car
una fermata	a bus stop
un'autostazione	a bus station
un orario	a schedule
arrivo	arrival
partenza	departure
coincidenza	connection
un biglietto	a ticket
nord	north
sud	south
est	east
ovest	west
prima classe	first class
seconda classe	second class
sottopassaggio	underpass
è libero questo posto?	Is this seat free?
è occupato/riservato?	Is it taken/reserved?
un volo	a flight
l'aereo	airplane
ho la prenotazione	I have a reservation
vorrei prenotare un posto	I would like to reserve a seat
il traghetto	ferry
l'aliscafo	hydrofoil
fumatori/non fumatori	smoking/non-smoking

SHOPPING

del pane	bread
del latte	milk
del burro	butter
una lattina (di)	a can (of)
dei biscotti	cookies
una mela	an apple
una pesca	a peach
dell'uva	grapes
un'arancia	an orange
una fetta di torta	a slice of cake

uno yogurt	yoghurt
una pasta	a cake, pastry
del profumo	perfume
un ombrello	umbrella
una cintura	belt
un disco	record
una cassetta	cassette
un libro	book
gli occhiali da sole	sunglasses
dei vestiti	clothes
un portachiavi	key ring

HEALTH

Body diagram labels: **la testa**, **l'occhio**, **l'orecchio**, **il naso**, **la spalla**, **la bocca**, **le braccia**, **il petto**, **lo stomaco**, **il ginocchio**, **la mano**, **la gamba**, **la caviglia**, **il piede**

la febbre	fever
un colpo di sole	sunburn
la puntura	sting
mal di denti	toothache
un medico	doctor
un dentista	dentist
una ricetta	prescription
sto male	I don't feel well
un ambulatorio	doctor's office
Pronto Soccorso	Emergency medical help
mi sono rotto(a) . . .	I have broken . . .
ho mal di . . .	I've got a pain in . . .

NUMBERS

0 **zero**		
1 **uno**	**primo**	first
2 **due**	**secondo**	second
3 **tre**	**terzo**	third
4 **quattro**	**quarto**	fourth
5 **cinque**	**quinto**	fifth
6 **sei**	**sesto**	sixth

7	sette	25	venticinque
8	otto	26	ventisei
9	nove	27	ventisette
10	dieci	28	ventotto
11	undici	29	ventinove
12	dodici	30	trenta
13	tredici	31	trentuno
14	quattordici	32	trentadue
15	quindici	40	quaranta
16	sedici	50	cinquanta
17	diciassette	60	sessanta
18	diciotto	70	settanta
19	diciannove	80	ottanta
20	venti	90	novanta
21	ventuno	100	cento
22	ventidue	200	duecento
23	ventitre	250	duecentocinquanta
24	ventiquattro		

PRICES

1,000 **mille lire**
1,500 **millecinquecento lire**
2,000 **duemila lire**
2,500 **duemilacinquecento**
3,000 **tremila lire**
3,500 **tremilacinquecento**
5,000 **cinquemila lire**
5,500 **cinquemilacinquecento**
10,000 **diecimila lire**
50,000 **cinquantamila lire**

DAYS AND MONTHS

lunedì	Monday	**venerdì**	Friday
martedì	Tuesday	**sabato**	Saturday
mercoledì	Wednesday	**domenica**	Sunday
giovedì	Thursday	**il lunedì**	on Mondays

gennaio	January	**luglio**	July
febbraio	February	**agosto**	August
marzo	March	**settembre**	September
aprile	April	**ottobre**	October
maggio	May	**novembre**	November
giugno	June	**dicembre**	December

COUNTRIES AND NATIONALITIES

L'Italia	Italy	**italiano(a)**	Italian
L'Inghilterra	England	**inglese**	English
La Scozia	Scotland	**scozzese**	Scottish
L'Irlanda	Ireland	**irlandese**	Irish

L'Irlanda del Nord	Northern Ireland		
Il Galles	Wales	**gallese**	Welsh
L'Olanda	Holland	**olandese**	Dutch
La Danimarca	Denmark	**danese**	Danish
Il Belgio	Belgium	**belga**	Belgian
Il Lussemburgo	Luxemburg	**lussemburghese**	Luxemburgian
La Germania	Germany	**tedesco(a)**	German
La Svizzera	Switzerland	**svizzero(a)**	Swiss
La Francia	France	**francese**	French
L'Australia	Australia	**australiano(a)**	Australian
Gli Stati Uniti	United States	**americano(a)**	American
La Spagna	Spain	**spagnolo(a)**	Spanish
Il Portogallo	Portugal	**portoghese**	Portuguese
La Grecia	Greece	**greco(a)**	Greek
Il Giappone	Japan	**giapponese**	Japanese
Il Canada	Canada	**canadese**	Canadian
L'Europa	Europe	**europeo(a)**	European

TIME

Ha l'ora?	Do you have the time?
un'ora	An hour
l'ora	the time (the hour)
una mezz'ora	half an hour
È l'una	It's 1 o'clock
Sono le due	it's 2 o'clock
Sono le tre e mezzo	It's three thirty
Sono le sei e un quarto	It's six fifteen
Sono le otto meno un quarto	It's a quarter to eight
Alle nove meno cinque	At five to nine
Alle quattro e venti	At twenty after four

WEATHER

Che tempo fa?	What is the weather like?
Fa caldo	It is hot
Fa freddo	It is cold
Piove	It is raining
Nevica	It is snowing
Fa bel tempo	It is a nice day
Fa brutto tempo	The weather is bad

sessantatre

COLORS
nero	black
bianco	white
verde	green
giallo	yellow
azzurro	blue
blu	dark blue
rosso	red
grigio	gray
marrone	brown
rosa	pink

CLOTHING SIZES

Shoes
U.S.

Women	5½	6½	7	7½	8	8½	9	10		
It	**35**	**36**	**37**	**38**	**38½**	**39**	**40**	**41**		

Men	6	6½	7	7½	8	8½	9	9½	10	10½	11
It	**39**	**40**	**40½**	**41**	**41½**	**42**	**42½**	**43**	**43½**	**44**	**45**

Women
U.S.	2	4	6	8	10	12	14
It	**36**	**38**	**40**	**42**	**44**	**46**	**48**

Men (suits)
U.S.	34	36	38	40	42	44	46
It	**44**	**46**	**48**	**50**	**52**	**54**	**56**

SOME ACRONYMS
AAST   **Azienda Autonoma di Soggiorno e Turismo** (Travel office)

EPT   **Ente Provinciale di Turismo** (Regional travel office)

FS   **Ferrovie dello Stato** (State Railways)

RAI   **Radio Televisione Italiana**

SIP   **Società italiana per l'esercizio telefonico** (Italian state telephone company)

ITALY
AND
THE ITALIANS

SVIZZERA
AUSTRIA
LE ALPI
LE DOLOMITI
FRANCIA
Lago Maggiore
Lago di Como
Lago di Garda
L. d'Iseo
SLOVENIA
CROAZIA
Bergamo
Milano
Venezia
Torino
il Po
Genova
Bologna
BOSNIA
Rimini
IL MARE ADRIATICO
Firenze
Pisa
San Marino
l'Arno
Siena
il Tevere
GLI APPENNINI
ROMA
Napoli
Bari
SARDEGNA
IL MAR TIRRENO
Cagliari
IL MARE MEDITERRANEO
Palermo
SICILIA
0 miles 100
0 kilometres 200

ITALY AND THE ITALIANS

Fact file

Italy, the "boot in the Mediterranean," with Rome as its capital, is bordered to the north by **Svizzera**, Switzerland, **Francia**, France, **Austria**, and **Slovenia**. The peninsula is washed on the eastern side by **il mare Adriatico**, the Adriatic Sea, and on the west by **il mar Tirreno**, the Tyrrhenian Sea. The islands of Sicily and Sardinia are in **il mare Mediterraneo** (*the Mediterranean*).

Mountains and rivers
Italy has three mountain ranges: **le Alpi, le Dolomiti,** and **gli Appennini**. The main rivers (**i fiumi**) are **il Po, l'Arno,** and **il Tevere** (*the Tiber*).

Islands
The largest of the Italian islands (**le isole**) are **la Sicilia** (*Sicily*) and **la Sardegna** (*Sardinia*). Other, smaller islands, which include Capri, Elba, and Ischia, also attract many thousands of visitors every year.

The Republic

Italy has only been a unified state since 1861. Before then, many regions of Italy had been ruled by Spain, Austria, or France. **Una repubblica** (*a republic*) since 1946, Italy now has **un presidente** (*a president*) and an elected parliament. Italy also contains two states within it. **La repubblica di San Marino** in **gli Appennini** is a small, independent state that issues its own postage stamps. It has its own mint and a small army of approximately 1,000.

La città del Vaticano (*Vatican City*) has been an independent state since 1929, although **la Chiesa cattolica** (*the Roman Catholic Church*) has been based in Rome for almost 2,000 years. **Il Papa** (*the Pope*), head of the Roman Catholic Church, is also head of this small, independent state.

Money

The Italian currency is the **lira** (in the plural, **lire**). The notes come in denominations of L1,000, L2,000, L5,000, L10,000, L50,000, and L100,000. The coins are L50, L100, L200, and L500.

The Regions

Italy is divided into 20 regions (**regioni**) and each region has **un capoluogo di regione** (*main town* or *city*). The 20 **regioni** are subdivided into **province** *(provinces)* and each **provincia** also has **un capoluogo di provincia**.

Towns and cities

The capital of Italy is **Roma** (*Rome*), which is in **Lazio**. Other major towns and cities are: **Milano** (*Milan*) in **Lombardia**, Italy's banking, insurance, industrial, and fashion center; **Torino** (*Turin*) in **Piemonte**, home of the Italian automotive industry; **Firenze** (*Florence*) in **Toscana**, which contains some of the most famous art treasures of the Renaissance; **Venezia** (*Venice*) in **Veneto**, built on small islands, with canals instead of streets; **Genova** (*Genoa*) in **Liguria**, the largest port in Italy; **Napoli** (*Naples*) in **Campania,** the "capital" of the south; **Bologna**, capital of **Emilia-Romagna**, known as **"la Grassa"** (*the fat one*), because of the region's tradition of good eating.

Over To You

Vehicle number plates indicate the province where the car was registered. For example, BO 134791: **BO** is for Bologna.

Look at the map on page 66 and the number plates. Can you figure out where each car was registered?

FI P28731	NA 840134	GE 673490
TO 489371	MI 019345	VE 749201

ANSWERS
Firenze; Napoli; Genova; Torino; Milano; Venezia.

Daily life in Italy

Banks (Banchi)

Banks are usually open Monday to Friday mornings from 8:30 A.M. until 1 P.M. They also open for an hour in the afternoon, usually from 3–4 P.M., although these times vary. The easiest and safest way to carry money is to use traveler's checks. You will need to show your passport when changing traveler's checks. The clerk will complete the necessary details on a form and will then tell you:

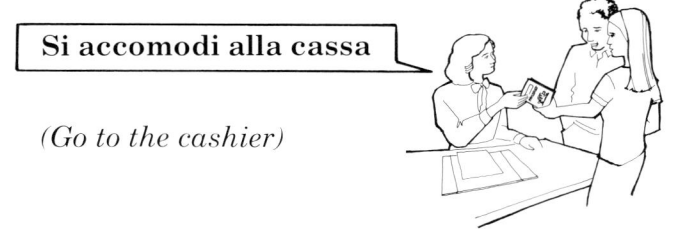

> **Si accomodi alla cassa**

(Go to the cashier)

Here you will be given your money.

The main banks are **Il Banco d'Italia, il Banco di Roma, la Cassa di Risparmio,** and **il Banco Nazionale del Lavoro**.

Shops (Negozi)

They usually open from 8:30 A.M. until 12:30 P.M. and from approximately 3 P.M. until 7:30 or 8 P.M. They are closed on Sundays and most stores are also closed on one other day of the week. The store's sign will indicate which day they have their **riposo settimanale** (*the day they are closed*).

You may also see the sign **Chiuso per ferie** on stores and also on *cafes* and movie theaters. This indicates that they are closed for their holidays.

Most Italian towns have **un mercato** (*a market*) where you can buy fresh fruit and other food. Although some towns now have **un supermercato** (*a supermarket*), usually outside the central area, many Italians still do most of their general shopping in **un alimentari** (*a general store*). Alternatively, you might want to visit different shops to buy specific items. **Una salumeria** sells cold meats and delicatessen products; **una panetteria** sells bread; **una pasticceria** sells pastry and cakes. Both bread and pastry are sold by weight. Incidentally, if you go to visit someone's home, it is the custom to take some pastry with you. **Una farmacia** sells medicine and other health products. For cosmetics, you should find **una profumeria**.

Finally, for fruit and vegetables, you should go to **un fruttivendolo,** for meat, you need to find **una macelleria**, and for books, you would look for **una libreria.**

Department stores

A sign saying **Entrata libera** indicates that you are welcome to go in and have a look around. However, in smaller shops, a salesperson is likely to approach you to ask what you would like.

Buongiorno. Desidera?	Good morning. Can I help you?
Sto guardando, grazie.	I'm just looking, thank you.

Department stores are usually to be found in cities and there are fewer of them than in many other countries. The names you will come across are **Standa, Upim, Coin,** and **La Rinascente**.

The sign **Saldi** in a shop window tells you that there is a sale on and this can be a good time to shop for clothes and shoes.

If you would like to try something on, you should ask **Posso provare?**

A dressing room is **un camerino**.

Finally, if you are buying presents, ask the salesperson to wrap them for you: **Mi può fare una confezione regalo, per favore?**

Post offices (La Posta)

They are usually open from 8 A.M. until 6:30 P.M., Monday to Saturday, although in smaller towns the post office will be closed on a Saturday. The post office usually has the sign **P&T** (**Poste e Telegrafi**) outside. If you are buying stamps, look for the window marked **Vendita Francobolli** or **Valori bollati**. However, it can be quicker to buy stamps at **una tabaccheria**.
If you want to send your letters by express mail, you will need to go to the post office. Look for the window marked **Espressi**.

Vorrei spedire questa lettera per Espresso

(I would like to send this letter express mail)

Another service that you might find useful is the **Fermo Posta**. Using this service, you can receive mail while in Italy. Letters should be addressed with your name, *Fermo Posta*, and then the name of the town or city where you will be picking up any mail.

SIMON HUGHES
FERMO POSTA
MESSINA

You will need to take your passport with you for identification purposes.

> **Buongiorno. E arrivata una lettera per me?**

(Good morning. Has a letter arrived for me?)

> **Il suo nome?**

(What is your name?)

> **Hughes**

> **Ha un documento?**

(Do you have any identification?)

Mail boxes are red or yellow. Outside the post office, there may be several to choose from: **Espressi** (*express mail*), **Stampe** (*newspapers*), **Per la città** (*local mail*), and **Per tutte le altre destinazioni** (*all other destinations*). If a mail box simply says **Lettere**, you can mail cards and letters for any destination. If you are looking for a mail box, ask: **Dove posso imbucare?** (*Where can I mail letters?*)

Telephones (Telefoni)

For long distance phone calls, it is a good idea to use **telefoni pubblici** (*public phone offices*). Operated by **SIP**, the Italian state-owned telephone company, these allow you to make your phone call and pay afterwards. You simply give the operator the number, including the town and country that you want to phone. The call will be placed for you.

Coin-operated phone booths take 100 and 200 lire coins as well as **gettoni** . The instructions for using a phone are usually accompanied by diagrams. However, the key instructions you need to understand are:

introdurre gettoni/monete (*put in gettoni/coins*)
sganciare il microtelefono (*lift the receiver*)
comporre il numero (*dial the number*)

For card phones, you will need to:

sganciare il microtelefono (*lift the receiver*)
inserire la carta (*insert the card*)
comporre il numero (*dial the number*)

Incidentally, before using your phone card, you need to remove the corner:

If you need to call the police or an ambulance, dial 113. These calls are free.

To phone the United States from Italy, dial 00 + 1, followed by the area code and the number. For example, to phone New York, dial 00 + 1 + 212, followed by the number. To phone Canada, follow the same procedure. To phone Great Britain from Italy, dial 00 + 44, then the area code without the first zero. It is cheaper to phone between 10 P.M. and 8 A.M. and all day on Sunday.

When Italians answer the phone, they say:

Pronto. Chi parla? (*Hello. Who is calling?*)

Over To You

You are in Rome. In which mail box should you mail these items?
(a) **STAMPE**
(b) **PER LA CITTÀ**
(c) **ESPRESSI**
(d) **PER TUTTE LE ALTRE DESTINAZIONI**

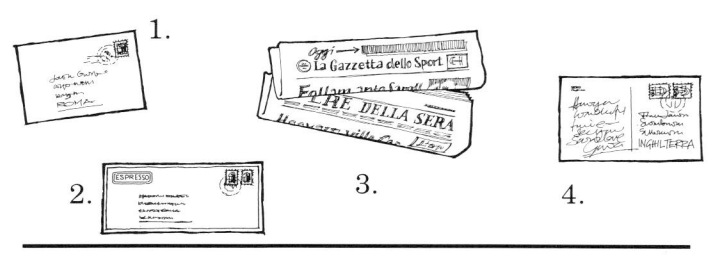

ANSWERS
1. = (b); 2. = (c); 3. = (a); 4. = (d).

Travel

1. Trains

The Italian state railways, **FS** (**Ferrovie dello Stato**), operate different types of trains and the price you pay can vary, depending on what train you are going to take. A **locale** is a slow train that usually stops at every station on its route; a **diretto** stops at most stations; an **espresso** stops at most main line stations; a **rapido** is a faster train, stopping only at major cities. On some trips, you will have to pay a supplement, and it is a good idea to reserve a seat. To travel on a **Super-Rapido Inter City** train, you will have to pay a supplement, as all the cars are first

> **Vorrei un biglietto per Venezia, con il rapido**
>
> *(I would like a ticket for Venice on the rapido)*

class. Reservations are also obligatory on these trains.

It may be worth finding out, if you are between 12 and 26, if you can buy **una carta verde**, which will give you either a 20% or 30% discount, depending on the time of year that you travel.

2. Buses and coaches

To travel by bus in Italian towns or cities, you must buy a ticket before you travel. **Biglietti** (*tickets*) can be bought from **un'edicola** (*a newspaper stand*) or where you see the **Tabacchi** sign. There is one price for single tickets, wherever you are traveling within the town or city. However, it is cheaper to buy **un blocchetto** (*a block of ten tickets*). When you get on the bus, stamp the ticket in the machine, which is usually near the door. It will probably be marked **convalida** or **obliterazione**. Failing to stamp your ticket can lead to **una multa** (*an on-the-spot fine*). You get on at the door marked **Entrata** and leave by the door marked **Uscita**. To check that you are getting off at the right stop, you ask:

> **Questa è la fermata per (la stazione)?**
>
> *(Is this the stop for [the station]?)*

To find out about travel by **pullman** *(coach)*, find the **autostazione** *(bus station)*. Here you will be able to pick up a schedule and, for longer trips, buy your ticket. Check the schedule carefully since there aren't many buses in some places, particularly on weekends. When you want to get off, make your way to the front of the bus and say to the driver:

> **Posso scendere?** *(Can I get off?)*

3. The subway

Rome and Milan have subways, **La Metropolitana**. You can buy **un biglietto semplice** *(a single ticket)* or **un carnet** *(a book of 10 tickets)*. Single tickets can be bought at ticket machines and books of tickets can be bought at **una tabaccheria**. You will also have to stamp your ticket as you do on the bus. Both subway systems have two lines: **Linea A** and **Linea B** in Rome and **Linea 1** and **Linea 2** in Milan. To find out which line you should take, ask:

> **Che linea è per (il Colosseo)?**

(Which line is it for [the Colosseum]?)

4. Air travel

The Italian national airline is **Alitalia**. Many of the main cities have an airport. The principal **aeroporti** *(airports)* are Roma, Milano, Bologna, Pisa, Venezia, Torino, Napoli, and Palermo.

Over To You

Split these phrases up in the correct places, and then match each person to the chosen form of transportation.

1. **Chelineaèperilforo?** (a)

2. **Unoperromaconilrapido.** (b)

3. **Midàunblocchetto.** (c)

4. **Possoscendere?** (d)

ANSWERS
1. Che linea è per il Foro? (c). 2. Uno per Roma, con il rapido (a). 3. Mi dà un blocchetto (d). 4. Posso scendere? (b).

Food and drink

1. Cafes and bars

Cafes and bars in Italy serve many purposes. They often have a telephone and many are combined with **una tabaccheria**. They serve alcoholic drinks, as well as coffee, tea, and soft drinks. You may also be able to buy snacks and ice cream. Many Italians have breakfast in a bar on their way to work: **un espresso** or **un cappuccino** and **un cornetto** *(a croissant)*.

settantanove 79

In some bars, you simply order and drink your drink **al bar** (at the bar):

Mi dà un espresso per favore

(I'll have an espresso, please)

In others, you pay for your drink **alla cassa** (at the cashier) and are given **uno scontrino** (a receipt). You then take your receipt to the barperson and tell him or her what you would like. You then drink your drink at the bar.

If you sit down **al tavolo** (at a table), **un cameriere** (a waiter) will take your order and bring it to your table. However, your drinks and snacks will cost more than if you stand at the bar, especially if you sit outside. The prices, **il listino prezzi**, are usually on display behind the bar and the prices for sitting at a table are marked **tavola**. Bars are often the only place where you will find a public restroom. To find out, you ask:

Scusi, c'è una toilette?

(Excuse me, is there a restroom?)

2. Eating out
The range of places to eat in Italy should ensure that there is something for everyone, from a simple **pizzeria** that only serves **pizze**, to a wide range of different **ristoranti** *(restaurants)*. In between, you will find *pizzerie* that also serve other meals and **trattorie** (a type of restaurant, which is usually quite informal). If eating in a restaurant, look for **il menù turistico**, which is a fixed-priced meal. Many restaurants, including pizzerie, charge for **pane e coperto** *(bread and cover)*, which you will find added to your bill. Incidentally, fast food has arrived in Italy and you will find American-style fast-food restaurants in many major cities.

3. Mealtimes
Many people don't eat **la colazione** *(breakfast)*; they just drink a cup of coffee in a bar on their way to work. However, everybody stops for **il pranzo** *(lunch)* and **la cena** *(dinner)*. The different courses are:
il primo piatto, first course, often soup or a pasta dish; **il secondo piatto,** main course, usually meat or fish. This is usually served with **un contorno** *(vegetable dish)*; **dolce o frutta** *(dessert)*, often a slice of cake or ice cream, or fresh fruit.

Newspapers and magazines

Giornali *(newspapers)* can be bought **in edicola** *(at newspaper stands)*, where you can also buy **riviste** *(magazines)* and **cartoline** *(postcards)*. The main newspapers include *La Stampa, La Repubblica, Corriere della Sera,* and *il Messaggero*.

Television and radio

There are three state-owned television channels, **canali**, run by **Radio Televisione Italiana (RAI)**. The channels are **Raiuno, Raidue,** and **Raitre**. There are also several private television stations, which tend to have more commercial breaks. These include **Canale 5, Retequattro,** and **Italia Uno**. There are also three RAI radio stations, **RadioUno, RadioDue,** and **RadioTre** as well as a large number of private, commercial stations.

School

In Italy, young people from 11 to 14 attend **la scuola media**. They go to school six days a week, starting each day at around 8:30 and finishing at about 1:20. Schools do not have cafeterias, since school finishes before lunch. Italian schoolchildren have a three-month vacation in the summer, as well as breaks at Christmas and Easter.

Homework is usually spent going over the day's lessons and a system of continuous assessment is used to decide whether a student should move on to the next year. If a student is **bocciato/a**, or fails, he/she has to repeat the course.

At the end of the scuola media, at the age of 14, students take an exam called the **Diploma / Licenza della Terza Media**. If they pass, they go on to **la scuola media superiore** or to **il liceo** until they are 18. Very few students leave school at 14, and if a student is "borderline" between pass and fail, behavior, class tests, and attendance record are taken into consideration.

Sports and leisure

As the school does not usually offer organized sports, many students take part in some form of **dopo scuola** *(after school)* activity. **Il calcio** *(soccer)*, **il tennis** *(tennis)*, **il ciclismo** *(cycling)*, and **il nuoto** *(swimming)* are all popular pastimes.

Sports are very popular in Italy, with one of the best-selling newspapers being **La Gazzetta dello sport**. The **Giro d'Italia** cycle race, second only in importance to the Tour de France, and auto racing, in particular, **Ferrari**, always attract a lot of interest and support.

But **il calcio** *(soccer)* is the most popular sport in Italy and **i tifosi** *(fans)* travel a long way to watch their teams play. The league matches are played on Sunday and for many people it is a day out. Some of the most successful teams of **Serie A** *(the top league)* are known by their colors: **i bianconeri** (black and white)—Juventus, from Torino

i rossoneri (red and black)—AC Milan
i nerazzurri (black and blue)—Inter, from Milan
i giallorossi (yellow and red)—Roma
gli azzuri (blue)—Napoli.
The Italian national team also plays in blue.

Going to the movies is also popular in Italy, whether it is to see Italian films or those from other countries. Foreign language films are usually **doppiati** *(dubbed)*. In addition, **fare un giro** *(going out for walk)* is popular with everyone and **fare una passeggiata** (going for a stroll in the main square or in the main street) is something that many people do. **La passeggiata** in the early evening is very popular and a great opportunity to meet friends, window-shop, or buy an ice cream.

Finally, family life is very important for most Italians and free time is often spent visiting with the family.

Meeting and greeting people

When you are introduced to a man, you should say **Buongiorno, Signor** and shake the person's hand. If you are being introduced to a woman, you should say **Buongiorno, Signora** (**Buongiorno** literally means "good day"). After 5 P.M. people generally say **Buonasera**. Family and close friends greet each other with a kiss on each cheek.

At the beginning of a meal, Italians will say **Buon appetito**. You should respond **Grazie, altrettanto** *(Thank you, the same to you)*. If you are staying with a family, you might be told: **Non fare complimenti** *(Don't stand on ceremony, or Make yourself at home)*.

On your friends' birthdays, you should wish them

Buon compleanno

(Happy birthday)

As Italy is a Catholic country, many people are named after saints, in the Catholic tradition. On the feast day of "their" saint, they celebrate their **onomastico** *(name day)*. On this day, you should wish them **Buona festa** and as for any special occasion, you should wish them **Auguri** *(best wishes)*.

Feeling ill

If you are not feeling well, you should pay a visit to a **farmacia**. You will be advised on what do, or on any medication to take and will probably not need to see a doctor. In an emergency, the numbers of the **Guardia Medica** *(doctors on duty)* are printed in the local paper. If possible, tell the **farmacista** *(the pharmacist)* what is wrong. Remember that sign language can also be very effective!

Ho mal di testa — *(I have a headache)*

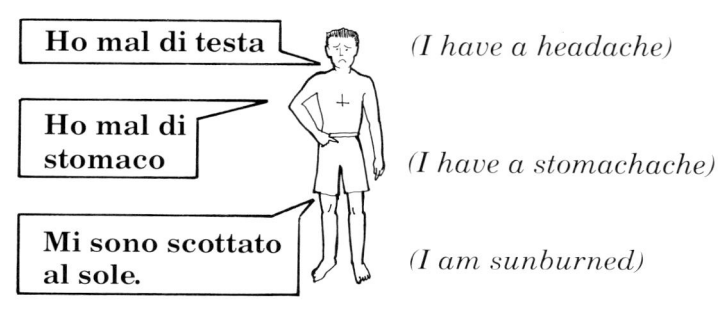

Ho mal di stomaco — *(I have a stomachache)*

Mi sono scottato al sole. — *(I am sunburned)*

Traffic warning

You must pay special attention when crossing the street as some drivers ignore **le strisce pedonali** *(pedestrian crossings)* and some even ignore **il semaforo** *(traffic lights)*.

Difficulties

If you have any problems, it is a good idea to be able to attract attention as quickly as possible. In case of an accident, you could shout:

Chiami la polizia!	Call the police!
Chiami un medico!	Call a doctor!
Presto!	Quick!

If someone is pestering you, tell the person:

Mi lasci in pace!   Leave me alone!

To draw attention to the situation, shout:

Aiuto!	Help!
Attenzione!	Look out!

If you've gotten this far into the book, then you must be interested in visiting Italy, So, where should you go?

In vacanza (On vacation)

1. Seaside resorts and the Lakes

As nowhere in Italy is far from the sea, there is a good variety of seaside resorts for you to visit, from **Rimini** to **Capri**. In the summer months Italian beaches can get very busy and you have to pay to use the facilities. The items you might want to rent are **una sdraia** *(a deck chair)*, **un ombrellone** *(a large umbrella)*, **un pedalò** *(a paddle boat)*, or **un lettino** *(a chaise lounge)*.

To ask for these, simply say **Vorrei** + the name of the item:

Vorrei un ombrellone e una sdraia

(I would like a large umbrella and a deck chair)

You will probably pay for the beach equipment for the whole day, **tutto il giorno**. However, **un pedalò, una bicicletta** *(a bicycle)*, or **un windsurf**, can usually be rented by the hour, **l'ora**.

Vorrei un pedalò. Quanto costa?

(I would like to hire a paddle boat. How much is it?)

Quindicimila l'ora

(15,000 (lire) per hour)

You could also ask to rent an item **per un'ora sola** *(for one hour only)*.

Vorrei una bicicletta per un ora sola   *(I would like to rent a bike for one hour only)*

The Italian Lakes, of which **Lago Maggiore** is the largest, are also a popular destination for many tourists. **Lago di Como, Lago di Garda,** and **Lago d'Iseo** are just three of the most popular lakes.

2. Skiing
If you prefer to take your vacation in the winter, you will find **le stazioni di sci** *(ski resorts)* in the Dolomites, in the Alpi, and even on the volcano Mount Etna!
Some package vacations will provide you with accommodations, **le lezioni di sci** *(ski lessons)*, and **lo ski pass**. You may, however, need to rent some equipment: **gli sci ed i bastoncini** *(skis*

and *ski poles)* and **gli scarponi** *(ski boots)*.
If renting equipment, you will probably need
to leave **un documento** (a means of
identification—like a passport or an ID card)
which you will be able to collect when you return
the equipment. And don't forget to take out extra
vacation insurance before you go.

> **Vorrei noleggiare degli sci e dei bastoncini**

(I would like to rent skis and ski poles)

> **Vorrei noleggiare degli scarponi**

(I would like to rent some ski boots)

While skiing, if you hear someone shouting **Fate largo!** or **Attenzione!**, make sure you get out of the way. The first means *Get out of the way!* and the second means *Look out!*

Over To You

Look at the map on page 66. Which of these items would you rent on vacation in the Dolomiti and which would you rent for a vacation in Rimini?

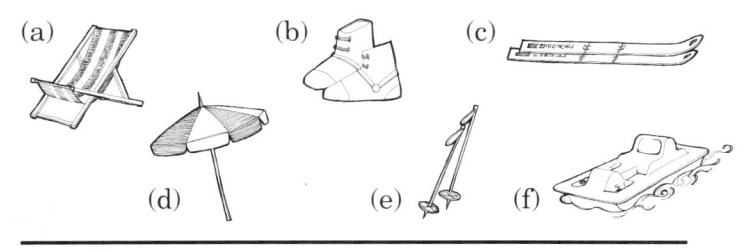

(a) (b) (c) (d) (e) (f)

ANSWERS (a) (d) and (f): Rimini; (b) (c) and (e): Dolomiti.

3. Towns and Cities

Italy's cities (**Le città**) give you an insight into its rich and varied past. Here are some examples:

Rome: With a history dating back more than 2,000 years, Rome contains an amazing collection of monuments, art, and architecture covering most of the last 2,000 years. There are many places to visit and it would require several visits to see all the main attractions. Here are some of the most popular:

Il Foro Romano (*the Forum*) and **il Colosseo** (*the Colosseum*), dating from Ancient Rome.
Il Campidoglio (*Capitoline Hill*), once the center of Ancient Rome, and **la Piazza del Campidoglio**, redesigned by Michelangelo.
La Piazza di Spagna and **la scalinata** (*Spanish Steps*).
La Città del Vaticano and **La Basilica di San Pietro** (*St Peter's*).
La Cappella Sistina (*the Sistine Chapel*), famous for its magnificent ceiling painted by Michelangelo.
La Fontana di Trevi (*the Trevi fountain*). It is said that if you throw a coin in the fountain, you will return to Rome.

Firenze (*Florence*): The capital of Tuscany contains many art treasures. The principal art galleries are **la Galleria degli Uffizi** and **il Palazzo Pitti**. However, they are both very big and you will not see everything even if you go every day for a week.

Pisa: Most famous for **la Torre Pendente** (*the Leaning Tower*).

Venice: The city built on small islands, with canals instead of roads. The best way to see Venice is to walk or to take **un vaporetto** (*a water bus*). This way, you will be able to catch a glimpse of some of the many **palazzi** (*palaces*) that line **il Canal Grande**.

Be warned. Every day thousands of visitors flock to the center of Venice and plans are being made to limit the number of visitors, possibly by putting a limit on the number of tourists allowed into the city each day.

Ercolano e Pompei: Herculaneum and Pompeii were destroyed when **Vesuvio** (*Vesuvius*) erupted in 79 A.D. and covered the towns in volcanic mud. Following excavation, you can now see the remains of these two towns, including plaster casts of some of the inhabitants. The volcanic ash preserved the human shape of the bodies, creating a mold. These have now been replaced by plaster casts that were taken during the excavation.

Siracusa: Siracuse, in Sicily, once the center of the ancient Greek world.

There are, of course, many other places of great interest to visit in Italy. However, remember that sight-seeing can be very tiring, especially in the hot summer months. It is a good idea to carry bottles of water with you, to combat the heat.

Le feste (Festivals)

Most towns and cities in Italy have their own **festa** (*a festival*), perhaps religious, historic, or to celebrate local food specialities. Here are two of the most well-known:

Siena: Il Palio takes place twice a year, in July and August. It is a horse race around the Piazza del Campo between riders from the ancient districts of the city. Dressed in medieval costume, they race to win the **Palio** *(banner)*.

Venice: Carnevale *(Carnival)* takes place over the five days before Ash Wednesday.

Where to stay

1. Campsites
Italy has a good variety of campsites. If you like to have all facilities provided, you will find that there are large campsites with **uno spaccio** *(a store)*, **un ristorante** *(a restaurant)*, **una lavanderia** *(laundry facilities)*, **una discoteca** *(a disco)*, **una piscina** *(a swimming pool)*, **il ciclismo** *(cycling)*, and water sports.

For information on camping, write to: Italian Federation of Camping and Caravaning (Federcampeggio), PO Box 23, 11 Via Vittorio Emanuele, 50041 Calenzano (Firenze).

2. Youth hostels

Ostelli della gioventù *(youth hostels)* provide relatively low-cost accommodations for anyone who is a member of the International Youth Hostel Association. The hostels come in all shapes and sizes, some of which, for example, Castroreale, in Sicily, and Montagnana, in Veneto, are set in beautiful locations.

They are supervised by **albergatori** *(innkeepers)*. Some have kitchens for the use of guests; others provide low-cost meals.

When you arrive, you will be asked:

| **Avete una tessera?** | *(Do you have a membership card?)* |

For more information on youth hotels, write to Associazione Italiana Alberghi per la Gioventù, Via Cavour 44, 00184 Roma.

3. Hotels

The cheapest type of hotel is **una locanda**. These are fairly basic and more common in the south of Italy. A hotel is either **un albergo** or **una pensione**. Hotels are graded using a star system: the more stars a hotel has, the more facilities it has (and probably the more expensive it will be). Some hotels offer **pensione completa** *(full board)*, **mezza pensione** *(half board)*. If you would like to receive information on hotels, write to the relevant local or regional tourist board. Here is an example of a letter.

> Spettabile Direzione,
>
> Avrei intenzione di visitare (Venezia) nel mese di agosto. Vi sarei grato(a) se voleste inviarmi una lista degli alberghi (dei campeggi/degli ostelli per la gioventù).
>
> Vi ringrazio in anticipo,
>
> Distinti saluti

> Dear Sir/Madam,
>
> I intend visiting (Venice) during the month of August. I would be grateful if you could send me a list of hotels (campsites/youth hostels).
>
> Thanking you in advance,
>
> Sincerely,

Making the most of your time!

Italy is a wonderful country to visit. To help you make the most of it, it can be a good idea to give yourself a fairly relaxed schedule so that visits to galleries, churches, and palazzi are interspersed with refreshment breaks, ice cream, and opportunities to sit, perhaps on the steps of the **Duomo** *(Cathedral)* in Florence or on the **scalinata** *(Spanish Steps)* in Rome, and watch the world go by.

Quiz

How much to do you remember? How many of these questions can you answer without looking back through this section of the book?

1. Look at these pictures. Where are these people going?

   (a) Dolomiti or Rimini?
   (b) Etna or Rimini?

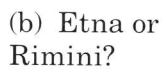

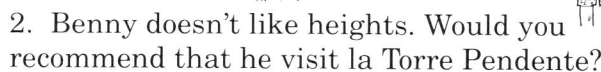

2. Benny doesn't like heights. Would you recommend that he visit la Torre Pendente?

3. Your friend is trying to call home with a phone card, but it won't work. Why not?

4. You are changing money in a bank and the clerk says:
Si accomodi alla cassa. Is he telling you to
   (a) take a seat?
   (b) go to the cashier?

5. You have decided to spend a lazy day on the beach. Which will be of more use to you?
   (a) **un lettino?**
   (b) **un pedalò**

6. Which doesn't belong, and why?
Il Tevere   **L'Arno**   **Le Dolomiti**

7. Why would you be surprised if your host offered you **un contorno** for breakfast?

8. On your last evening in Italy, your friend invites you to **fare una passeggiata**. Will you need any special equipment?

ANSWERS
For the answers to these questions look at the following pages:
1. 66 & 87–8, 2. 91, 3. 75, 4. 70, 5. 87, 6. 67, 7. 81, 8. 84.

You are now ready to set off to Italy. **Buon viaggio!**